PREHISTORIC PARK

with Nigel Marven

Adapted by Susan Evento
Designed by Matthew Eberhart, Evil Eye Design, Inc.

Meredith® Books
Des Moines, Iowa

© 2006 FremantleMedia North America, Inc.
Prehistoric Park is a trademark of Impossible Pictures Ltd.
Based on the television program *Prehistoric Park* produced by Impossible Pictures Ltd.
Licensed by FremantleMedia Licensing Worldwide.
www.fremantlemedia.com

2006 Meredith Corporation
Reprinted in perfect bound tradepaper format 2007.
All rights reserved.
Manufactured and printed in China.
First Edition
ISBN 978-0-696-23691-4 (perfect bound)
ISBN 978-0-696-23533-7 (saddle stitch)

We welcome your comments and suggestions. Write to us at:
Meredith Books, 1716 Locust St., Des Moines, IA 50309-3023

Visit us at meredithbooks.com

CONTENTS

A Theme Park with an EXTINCT TWIST

What if the amazing animals that time has left behind could be brought back to the present and given a second chance? Wildlife adventurer Nigel Marven plans on doing just that! He will plunge into prehistory to rescue creatures on the brink of extinction and bring them back to the safety of Prehistoric Park.

As Nigel travels way, way back to prehistoric periods, he will rush against time to avoid meteorites and exploding volcanoes. He will brave the cold of the Ice Age and the slime of prehistoric swamps to save such magnificent beasts as the T. rex, the woolly mammoth, and the Arthropleura. And if that's not daring enough, Nigel will have to lure these often gigantic and dangerous animals through the time portal into Prehistoric Park. He certainly has his work cut out for him!

TEAM NIGEL

Nigel has a crew that will assist him in carrying out his plan. He has people who will travel with him through the time portal into prehistoric times and back. And he has others who will stay at the park, getting it ready for the animals and taking care of the animals once they arrive.

Two of Nigel's most important crew members are Bob and Suzanne. Suzanne is a veterinarian who will use her medical skills and knowledge to help keep Prehistoric Park's creatures happy and healthy. Bob, the head park keeper, oversees the people who build the pens and maintain the park. He will also be Suzanne's assistant when it comes to caring for the animals. Bob and Suzanne must always stay on their toes, because, as you will see, Nigel often brings back big surprises to Prehistoric Park.

The Ultimate WILDLIFE SANCTUARY

If Nigel can make extinct animals feel at home anywhere, it's here. The sanctuary has everything they need. In terms of habitats, there's the ocean to the south and mountains to the north. There are savannah, forest, rivers, and even a waterfall. These are perfect environments for keeping prehistoric animals.

All they need now are the prehistoric creatures themselves. Nigel plans to bring back a few of each species at a time to see how they do in the 21st century.

In Search of the King:
T. rex
(TYRANNOSAURUS REX)

Nigel wants to start with the meanest and scariest of all extinct prehistoric creatures—Tyrannosaurus Rex. To rescue the last of the T. rex, Nigel must go back to the very end of the age of dinosaurs—about 65 million years ago.

The most widely accepted theory about why dinosaurs became extinct is that a meteorite smashed into Earth.

The crater is still visible in Mexico where the meteorite landed. Around that time, masses of T. rex lived in present-day Montana. But 65 million years ago, Montana looked nothing like it does today. There was no grass. Volcanoes dotted the landscape. There, the T. rex was king.

Can Nigel bring back the king?

65 MILLION YEARS AGO

Sighting
BIG BEAKS
(ORNITHOMIMUS)

Follow our trusty safari guide, Nigel, as he wanders through a 65 million-year-old forest in search of a T. rex. He is confident that it won't be too hard to track down a 45-foot-long, 5-ton monster!

Before long, Nigel spies pairs of three-toed tracks, tracks that tell him he is following dinosaurs that stand on two legs. Unfortunately, these tracks aren't big enough to be those of the monstrous T. rex. Other clues—nibbled leaves and broken twigs—point out that he is tracking a vegetarian dinosaur, not the flesh-eating T. rex.

Suddenly, Nigel hears rustling in the bushes. In a flash, he is staring at an ostrichlike dinosaur. It is an Ornithomimus, a dinosaur whose name means *bird mimic*. As Nigel sneaks closer to this creature, it rushes at him, screeching loudly. Nigel makes a hasty retreat from the warning sound. Soon, other Ornithomimus start popping their heads up all over the place.

Quick-thinking Nigel decides to capture an Ornithomimus using a technique that has worked successfully with ostriches. As he charges the herd, he attempts to single out one and place his sock over its head. As the birdlike dinosaur screeches and squirms, the rest of the herd flee. But something other than Nigel has sent them off in a panic.

DID YOU KNOW?

❖ Their full name is Ornithomimus velox (orn-ith-oh-MY-muss), and they are close relatives of the T. rex.

❖ Although Ornithomimus were vegetarians (they ate plant shoots), they wouldn't turn their beaks up at insects or bits of meat.

❖ Their long legs and somewhat hollow bones helped them turn instantly.

❖ It has been estimated from fossil tracks that these creatures could run 40 miles an hour or faster.

T. rex
Find Nigel

Now Nigel has something much, much bigger to deal with. He need not search for T. rex. They have found him!

As Nigel runs away, he takes some comfort in the fact that he has one advantage. Although T. rex can run about 25 miles an hour, they can't run that fast over uneven ground. They are so top heavy that if they trip and fall, they can kill themselves. Nigel sprints to the safety of a confined space, because he knows that the T. rex won't pursue him in such a small area. Nigel, our fearless guide, has had a close call!

As day one of the safari draws to a close, Nigel hasn't caught a T. rex or even an Ornithomimus. But he has certainly had a day full of adventure. It's not every day he gets to wrestle an Ornithomimus and outrun T. rex!

Waking Up to Three-Horned Faces—
OH, HORRIDUS!
(TRICERATOPS)

When Nigel straightens up from washing his face in the lake the next morning, he comes face-to-face with a herd of Triceratops! He finds these 8-ton, 25-foot-long creatures a glorious sight.

Not only is he inspired by their grandness, he is also excited by the fact that they are prey for T. rex. He knows that the T. rex can't be far away.

WHAT'S IN A NAME?

Triceratops horridus means horrible three-horned face. Its nearly 7-foot head was the biggest of any land animal. It had one horn over each eye and one above the nose. Perhaps the Triceratops used these horns for defense.

How to Take Home a T. rex

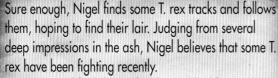

Sure enough, Nigel finds some T. rex tracks and follows them, hoping to find their lair. Judging from several deep impressions in the ash, Nigel believes that some T. rex have been fighting recently.

Soon Nigel finds himself in the middle of T. rex territory! As he sees two sparring, he throws himself behind a rock. The T. rex move off, and Nigel emerges from his hiding place to examine the bones strewn about. This must be where they bring their food to eat.

Nigel knows that it is one thing to find a T. rex, but quite another to get one back to Prehistoric Park. Fortunately, dinosaurs lay eggs, and Nigel hopes to find some, because that would make his job a lot easier. Among the remains of the T. rex victims, Nigel finds a T. rex nest. Unfortunately, he is too late. The shells are all empty. Either they have been broken into by a predator or they are last season's eggs.

Another day draws to a close, and our safari guide is still no closer to saving the T. rex. And in the sky above are the first signs that the meteorite is closing in. Shooting stars streak across the sky, and huge boulders plow into Earth's atmosphere at 20,000 miles an hour.

LEAN MEAN POWER MACHINES

T. rex had huge jaw muscles that gave them a bite (using serrated, banana-shape teeth) 10 times more powerful than a lion's. Although their arms were small, they were powerful. T. rex used them like forks to bring victims toward their jaws.

Two for the PRICE OF ONE?

As day three dawns, a pack of mean-looking T. rex show up, looking for trouble. They're after their favorite food, Triceratops. They're charging the herd, looking for the weakest one. As the Triceratops flee, a baby Triceratops runs the wrong way and is swept up by a female T. rex. But help is close at hand. As a large male Triceratops fights off the big female T. rex, she drops her prey. In the meantime, the male T. rex have left the female alone to fend for herself. So much for the pack watching out for her!

The Triceratops injures the T. rex's thigh and takes off. The injured T. rex spots another baby Triceratops. Nigel sets up the time portal, hoping to lure this baby Triceratops through, with the T. rex following. He waves his shirt like a matador waving a cape and is followed by the Triceratops, which charges into the portal. The T. rex, however, doesn't take the bait. Well, one out of two isn't bad. The Triceratops is Prehistoric Park's first prehistoric creature and also its first dinosaur!

Where There are Triceratops ...
T. rex Are Likely to Follow

Back to 65 million years ago . . . and this time Nigel is determined to find a T. rex! He spies lots of dinosaur tracks but spots one set that particularly interests him. The impressions look as if a T. rex has been dragging one of its legs, and Nigel believes that they were made by the injured T. rex. Nigel heads downstream, following her tracks. With any luck, she will have slowed down and he will be able catch up. Suddenly, he hears her echoing footfalls. It's impossible for a 5-ton animal to tread softly!

Using her superb sense of smell, the T. rex finds a Triceratops body in the water. She's hungry and desperate to get into the water to grab the Triceratops, but she won't risk going into the fast-flowing water that might flip her over. The hungry, injured female limps off, leaving Nigel to figure out what to do next.

TIME
Is Running Out!

Nigel and his crew work their way downriver just ahead of the T. rex. She won't walk onto uneven land and she doesn't like going near the water. So Nigel and the other crew members build a wooden wall to direct her straight toward the time portal.

It's now or never. The meteorite is getting closer. And so is the T. rex. A herd of Ornithomimus, spooked by the appearance of the T. rex, are running scared. The Ornithomimus find themselves trapped between the T. rex and the 21st century. What choice do they have? The herd scurry through the time portal to Prehistoric Park. Oh my, a baby Ornithomimus, confused and slower than the rest, gets caught by the injured T. rex!

WILL T. REX FOLLOW
a Sandwich?

The injured T. rex, carrying the Ornithomimus baby, is now traveling so slowly that Nigel catches up. He follows her cautiously to a nest of her babies. The babies are very hungry, and that's why she has carried the Ornithomimus uphill all this way. Out of nowhere, a male T. rex appears on the scene and he is eagerly eyeing the Ornithomimus. The T. rex young are hiding. If he sees them, they could be in trouble. Like other reptiles, T. rex can be cannibalistic.

The female fights the male and succeeds in protecting her babies, but she loses the battle for the food. As the male walks away with his prize, hundreds of miles away the meteorite finally enters Earth's atmosphere. The shock wave is only three minutes away, and Nigel must do some very quick thinking! In a flash, he sets up the portal and lures the babies with the only thing available—a meat sandwich! They greedily follow the scent of food and . . . they are rescued!

Meanwhile...
BACK AT THE PARK

The Triceratops, named Theo, has been in a pen near the river. Grass wasn't around when it lived in prehistoric times, so Bob has placed him in an area where he can browse on low shrubs and trees. To grow to 8 tons, Theo will have to spend most of his life eating!

One morning, Bob and Suzanne notice that the previously happy Theo is starting to display some strange behavior. He is butting his head repeatedly against a tree.

Suzanne sees that his frill has changed color and thinks that he is entering adolescence. They agree that Theo needs a target for his aggression, and Bob thinks he has a good plan.

The other newcomers are also getting used to Prehistoric Park. The excitable herd of Ornithomimus is busy checking out its new grassy pen. The brother and sister T. rex, Terrence and Matilda, are eating huge chunks

of meat while being watched in an observation pen.

Bob soon reveals his plan. He heads toward Theo's pen, driving a tractor covered with horns and tires for padding. Nigel joins him in the fun on the tractor as they joust with Theo. This is just the thing Theo needs to let off some steam. It's not another Triceratops, but it's the next best thing!

Nigel's dream of having a park filled with prehistoric creatures he has saved from extinction is beginning to take shape!

The unstoppable Nigel is already planning his next adventure. He has decided to travel back to the end of the Ice Age to rescue one of the most famous of all extinct animals—the woolly mammoth. But who knows what else he might run across and bring back to Prehistoric Park in his travels?

No Place for a
MAMMOTH
(MAMMUTHUS SUBPLANIFRONS)

Nigel is back at the end of the Ice Age—10,000 years ago, when mammoths were struggling to survive. The warming of the climate has already changed the world. It is still cold, but the ice is receding north, and the mammoths are following it. The last surviving mammoths were found in Siberia, and that's where Nigel is. Where he stands now is dense forest. It was once rich, open grassland, covered with huge herds of grazing mammoths. Finding the last ones living will not be an easy task.

LET SLEEPING BEARS LIE!

While trudging through miles and miles of dense forest, Nigel stumbles upon a prehistoric cave and can't resist exploring it. He soon retreats hastily with a cave bear close behind! He has chosen the wrong creature to disturb.

After emerging from its cave, the bear stands up—all three-quarter tons and 13 feet of him! Wisely, Nigel runs for a tree and scrambles up it. Although Nigel knows bears don't climb trees, he didn't know that bears were around at the end of the Ice Age.

FAST FACTS

Mammoth dung isn't really all that gross. Well, you'll have to take Nigel's word for it, because he stuck his finger in it! Like elephants, mammoths can't digest plant cellulose. The plant vegetation goes through mammoths virtually unchanged. That's why they have to feed for 16 hours a day.

WHERE THERE'S DUNG

Nigel has decided that the best way to catch a mammoth is to get up high and scout the terrain. But all he can see are trees, trees, and more trees. Mammoths need plains and grasslands, and there's none of that anywhere. The changing habitat is just one reason that Nigel is finding it difficult to spot a mammoth. By this time, mammoths are also hunted by Ice Age humans.

Nigel finally locates a spot at the base of the mountains and wanders there, hoping to find a mammoth. Out of the corner of his eye, he spots a mammoth tusk gleaming in the snow. As Nigel digs it out, he notices that it has been carved into an instrument. Are Ice Age people close by? Are woolly mammoth still around? Before long, he sees massive footprints and then a concrete clue that the mammoth can't be far away. He discovers a mound of dung . . . and it's still warm!

A MAMMOTH
Is Down!

Nigel finds two mammoths. One of them is lying in a pit, not moving. Nigel knows that Ice Age humans caught creatures by covering pits with snow and then spearing the animals after they fell in.

The mammoth staying by her dead herd mate is making a grumbling sound, trying to communicate with her. It's likely that the dead mammoth is her sister. The standing mammoth has also been injured. The poor thing looks sick—her head is down, and her ears are close to her head. She's so weak, she can hardly lift her trunk. Nearby, Nigel finds a broken spear and thinks its tip must have broken off in the mammoth's hide. He knows that if he and his team don't treat the infected wound, this mammoth will also die.

Nigel's team gives her a shot of antibiotics, and Nigel stays with her throughout the night to protect her from Ice Age hunters and other predators. It's a long night. Although the Ice Age hunters want to claim their prize, they skirt around the edge of the forest but come no closer. The prospect of getting a meal attracts some other unwanted visitors too. The fearless Nigel chases off wolves and keeps hyenas at bay. By dawn, the mammoth is able to get up, and Nigel coaxes her away from her dead sister and through the time portal to Prehistoric Park.

DID YOU KNOW?

- Mammoths became extinct partially because of overhunting by early peoples.

- Female mammoths had dainty, straight tusks. The male mammoths, called bulls, had much bigger tusks that ended in a corkscrew.

Meanwhile...
BACK AT THE PARK

Because the Ornithomimus look like ostriches, Bob places them in a grassy area. But they won't eat the grass! On closer scrutiny, Bob notices that the Ornithomimus don't have any teeth and that the insides of their mouths feel like sandpaper, much like that of ducks or geese. So Bob moves them to an enclosure with their own pond and hopes they will find food there that's more to their liking.

While the Ornithomimus won't eat anything, the T. rex have been polishing off everything in sight! They've been gobbling up huge chunks of meat!

Although the mammoth has made it back to Prehistoric Park, she is in serious need of help. Suzanne hasn't nursed a mammoth before, but she's hoping that what she knows about elephants will help. After sedating the mammoth, Suzanne works carefully to treat her wound. She's trying to remove the spear tip, but it's not easy, because mammoths have a really thick layer of fat beneath the skin to keep them warm in the Ice Age. Finally, with the spear tip removed, the mammoth is back on her feet and hopefully on the road to recovery. The team decides to call her Martha.

Soon, all of Prehistoric Park's creatures are enjoying their food, except for Martha. During the next couple of days, she doesn't eat a thing. If she doesn't eat soon, she's not going to make it.

In Search of PREHISTORIC SALAD

Nigel decides to go back to the beginning of the Ice Age (150,000 years ago), when the mammoths were flourishing, to find out what they were eating.

Unlike the last trip, Nigel finds himself in the full grip of the Ice Age. It's colder and there aren't any trees, but there are lots of different types of grasses.

Before long, Nigel sees a mammoth matriarch and her herd. There are mothers and calves—a whole extended family. He observes that they all follow the matriarch. They stop when she stops, they sleep when she sleeps, and they eat and drink when she does. They all seem to be thriving on their grassy diet.

Suddenly, there's a commotion in the herd. It's a male (bull mammoth), and he's looking for a female to mate with. He's very aggressive. The matriarch starts to lead the herd away from him.

Between a Rock
(BULL MAMMOTH)
and a Hard Place
(ELASMOTHERIUM)

Nigel starts to scoop up grasses, mosses, and twigs to bring back to Prehistoric Park to tempt Martha to start eating. While collecting the vegetation, Nigel observes another creature eating the rich vegetation of the grassland. It's an Elasmotherium, a prehistoric rhinoceros. At first, because of its poor eyesight, the Elasmotherium doesn't see Nigel, but Nigel knows it's only a matter of time before the creature smells him. And when the Elasmotherium does get close enough to see Nigel, it'll charge with that deadly horn—nearly 7-feet long. Ouch!

Nigel drops the bag of vegetation as he finds himself between the bull mammoth and the Elasmotherium. He can either be trampled by the angry bull mammoth or charged by the equally frightening Elasmotherium. Quick-footed Nigel runs and jumps on his snowmobile and narrowly escapes both beasts!

He returns to pick up his bag of vegetation and uses his binoculars to view the Elasmotherium from a distance. He decides to go back, set up the time portal, and use himself as bait to lure the Elasmotherium back to Prehistoric Park.

Nigel, who set out only to get some prehistoric salad, returns with a prehistoric rhinoceros weighing several tons! Won't Bob and Suzanne be surprised?

Martha, THE LONELY MAMMOTH

Even with prehistoric salad, Martha isn't tempted to eat. What's wrong with her? From what Nigel saw of mammoth behavior while visiting prehistoric times, he thinks that she might be lonely. After all, she's a herd animal. She probably needs some company.

Since orphaned elephants have been put in with established herds in the past, Nigel decides to put an elephant matriarch in with Martha to see if they bond. If they do, Nigel can bring over the rest of the elephant herd. It's a real risk, because elephant matriarchs have

been known to kill elephants trying to come into the herd. But it's a chance they have to take if they want to save Martha.

Bob, Nigel, and Suzanne introduce the elephant to Martha. These two magnificent creatures look at one another through a fence. Martha smells the matriarch and then approaches her with her trunk in a gesture of friendship. Bob opens the gate, and soon Martha has a new extended family of elephants.

Mysterious Dinosaurs, FLYING REPTILES
(PTEROSAURS)

Nigel travels back to the forests of prehistoric China, 125 million years ago, in search of a dinosaur with four feathery wings—the Microraptor.

Nigel's crew is in a remote area of China with active volcanoes that are about to erupt. Explosions and hot, flowing lava aren't the only dangers they face, however. Active volcanoes seep carbon dioxide gas, which can be dangerous at high concentrations. This gas can't be seen or smelled, so it's hard to know when the concentration is rising. The best way to avoid suffocating from the gas is to seek higher ground.

Nigel and his team set up camp at a freshwater lake, and it's not long before they see flying reptiles—pterosaurs. Wow! A group of them is fishing in the lake. The pterosaurs swoop low, close to the surface, with their jaws skimming the water. When something in the water moves, they snap their jaws shut like a trap.

Later, the team returns to the camp, only to find that everything has been destroyed. And all of their food—including meat—has been eaten. Luckily, one of Nigel's crew members has a knapsack with some food in it, but that's all they have left to eat.

Don't Ruffle
HIS FEATHERS
(INCISIVOSAURUS)

Nigel and his team are on the trail of the Microraptor, but something is on their trail too. He and his cameraperson try to get closer to see if the creature following them is their camp wrecker. Oh, no! It smacks right into the camera lens. Ugh! It has left dinosaur snot and spit all over the camera. Luckily, the creature doesn't attack and soon it's nibbling on some ferns. This indicates to the team that it's a vegetarian, not the meat-eating creature that wrecked their camp. And it's not the Microraptor they were looking for either. Although it has feathers like the Microraptor does, it has buckteeth, which the Microraptor doesn't. Nigel pursues the bucktoothed wonder, but it jumps into the air and gets away. All Nigel has succeeded in doing is ruffling its feathers—feathers that apparently weren't used for flight.

All of a sudden, Nigel hears screams. Four small dinosaurs are attacking the crew member who has the knapsack of food. As Nigel's team fights them off, the dinosaurs run off with the knapsack. The camp wreckers have struck again!

Just when Nigel has about given up hope of catching Microraptors for his park, he sees one gliding from tree to tree. Ah, and there's more than one. There's a group of these agile pterosaurs, all moving in the same direction.

Suddenly, Nigel sees what they are following—titanosaurs. These vegetarians are huge creatures, sometimes weighing more than 20 tons! They're completely harmless, unless they tread on you! When the titanosaurs tramp through the forest, they turn over the soil and break down rotting logs, leaving a mess behind—grubs, insects, and worms. The Microraptors follow the titanosaurs and feed on the exposed insects.

MICRORAPTORS
Don't Disappoint

While the Microraptors are busy eating, Nigel tries to catch one, but he finds out that they are much quicker than he is. Microraptors don't flap their wings. They can't fly, but they can glide. They can't take off from the ground like a bird can, so they use their claws to climb trees and then they jump off, using their short feathers to help them glide to the ground.

Nigel has devised a plan to outwit his feathered friends. He and his crew set up walls made of nets to form a pen. Inside the pen, they dig up soil, exposing earthworms and other small creatures. They hope the Microraptors will swoop down into the trap to eat but won't be able to get out, since they can't take off from the ground.

While the suspicious Microraptors are busy inspecting the trap, two bucktoothed wonders swoop in and destroy it. The Microraptors climb up into the trees and look down at Nigel and his crew.

Nigel and his crew return briefly to Prehistoric Park to stock up on food, research the bucktoothed animals they saw, and get a net gun to help them capture the wily Microraptors.

Back in prehistoric China, Nigel and his crew are on the lookout for signs of increasing volcanic activity. They have carbon dioxide monitors, and if the levels become too high, they have gas masks to wear.

Is It a Bird or A DINOSAUR?
(INCISIVOSAURUS)

Nigel and his crew run into the bucktoothed creatures again. While back in the park, Nigel learned that these were Incisivosaurus, creatures halfway between dinosaurs and birds. The male is displaying his beautifully colored feathers to a female, just like modern male birds do to their mates.

FAST FACTS

Feathers probably first evolved to keep dinosaurs warm. Some dinosaurs, like the Incisivosaurus, used them for display. Feathers that allowed animals to take flight evolved much later.

SLEEPING DRAGONS THAT WON'T WAKE UP (MEI LONG)

As Nigel and crew follow a herd of titanosaurs, they are heading downhill, toward the active volcano. Nigel comes across the camp wreckers. He knows that they are called Mei long, which means sleeping dragons. Nigel's carbon dioxide monitor suddenly makes a beep. The Mei long aren't sleeping—they've suffocated from the deadly gas!

Nigel and crew scramble toward higher ground, but before long, the fearless Nigel decides they can't give up on saving more creatures from the eruption. As he and his crew follow the trail back down, they find a nest of eggs.

The soil, warmed by the volcanic activity, is the perfect incubator.

Here comes another tremor! The ground shakes. Soon, titanosaurs head for their eggs, with Microraptors following close behind. Nigel uses the net gun to catch several Microraptors. The volcano is erupting and it's spooking all the animals, even the big ones! The titanosaurs are heading toward Nigel. He sets up the time portal and brings the Microraptors and titanosaurs back to Prehistoric Park all at once!

A Prehistoric Park MENAGERIE

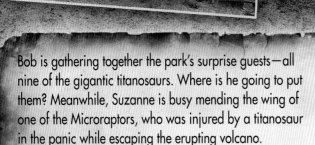

Bob is gathering together the park's surprise guests—all nine of the gigantic titanosaurs. Where is he going to put them? Meanwhile, Suzanne is busy mending the wing of one of the Microraptors, who was injured by a titanosaur in the panic while escaping the erupting volcano.

What's been going on with some of Prehistoric Park's other residents? There was a heat wave, and Martha the mammoth was finding it a bit hairy adjusting to the 21st century. It's not exactly the ideal climate for an Ice Age mammoth! The very woolly Martha received a much-needed summer makeover—a haircut.

The T. rex brother and sister, Terence and Matilda, were hosed off and separated because they couldn't get along. Neither of them is very happy about this change in the living situation.

Although most of the Ornithomimus are happy in their new home away from home, one started to act strangely. She began sulking alone in the shade. It turned out that this is the behavior of an expectant mother, and indeed, she laid a nest full of eggs.

It's been a long and exciting two weeks, but things seem to be settling down—that is, until the next morning, when the park wakes up to the pitter-patter of tiny, three-toed baby Ornithomimus. And things will become even more hectic, because Nigel is busy planning his next safari and thinking about the ferocious cats and flesh-eating birds he will bring back to Prehistoric Park!

Weird and Wonderful CREATURES

DID YOU KNOW?

- Saber-toothed cats could run at an amazing speed, but only for short distances.

- Their stocky front legs helped them bring down and hold massive animals, like the Toxodon.

- Saber-toothed cats could eat 110 pounds of meat in one sitting!

On this trip, Nigel is going back to prehistoric South America in search of ferocious cats and giant killer birds! Before 1 million years ago, South America had been cut off from the rest of the world for more than 30 million years. All sorts of huge, unusual creatures were able to evolve—animals not found anywhere else on the planet! But by 1 million years ago, a land bridge had formed between North and South America.

One of the most wonderful creatures from that time, which Nigel wants to save from extinction, is the saber-toothed cat. Since Nigel was a kid, his most prized possession has been a saber-toothed skull. Its teeth are truly awe-inspiring. It is thought that this cat used its oversize canines to bite its prey's throat, crushing its windpipe in one devastating bite! A million years ago, these fierce cats were the top predators of North America. As they spread into South America, they quickly took over the hunting grounds of the strangest predators the world has ever known—the 10-foot-tall killer bird called the terror bird.

Even for bird-loving Nigel, catching the 10-foot terror bird might be a difficult task. But, when Nigel sets his mind to something, there's not much that can stop him!

When Nigel and his team arrive in South America, the saber-toothed cats are thriving, but the terror birds are struggling to survive. What other weird and wonderful creatures will Nigel encounter as he enters this amazing time period?

Prehistoric
ALL-TERRAIN ANIMALS
(TOXODONS)

It doesn't take Nigel and his crew long to find some peculiar beasts. As they exit the time portal, Nigel's jeep plunges into the midst of a herd of Toxodon! The ears, eyes, and nostrils of these strange animals are positioned high on their heads so they can spend a lot of time partially submerged in water.

Nigel thinks the Toxodon look and act similar to modern-day hippos; they are vegetarians and wallow in water in the heat of the day. And he suspects that, like hippos, these large eating machines might be dangerous. Nigel is s-o-o-o-o right! While Nigel admires the Toxodons lazing in the water, one charges him from behind. Nigel runs and jumps into his jeep, with the Toxodon not far behind. Although this creature weighs about two tons, it is fast. Fortunately, this prehistoric all-terrain animal isn't able to outrun Nigel's jeep!

Nigel then spots a saber-toothed cat that's charging a Toxodon. For the poor Toxodon, the attack is over quickly. Other saber-toothed cats, including cubs, fight over the meal, and yet they leave a lot of carcass behind. Walking away from food is a sure sign that the saber-toothed cats are thriving.

Flesh-Eating
BIRDS
(TERROR BIRDS)

Leaving fresh Toxodon meat around is a sure way of attracting South America's former top predator, the terror bird. And sure enough, before long, one shows up. However, once the terror bird sees a saber-toothed cat approaching, it drops the meat it's stealing and flees in a panic. Nigel sees firsthand that the saber-toothed cats are outcompeting the terror birds, and that's why the birds became extinct.

Nigel thinks the terror bird is the perfect specimen to take back to Prehistoric Park. But how will he get it there? Well, to Nigel, it's pretty straightforward. He must get the meat the terror bird dropped, even if that means getting dangerously close to the saber-toothed cat! Fortunately, the saber-toothed cat only looks up and roars at Nigel, so

once again, he manages to get away safely. Nigel uses a rope to tie the meat to his jeep and then drives through the time portal into Prehistoric Park, with the hungry terror bird sprinting behind.

Although Nigel has captured one of South America's most brutal predators, his mission is far from over. There's one final puzzle Nigel needs to solve. If saber-toothed cats were once America's top predators, how did they end up losing the fight for survival? Nigel decides to return to South America about 10,000 years ago, when the last saber-toothed cats were roaming its vast plains. He has invited Saba Douglas-Hamilton, a big cat expert, to join him in tracking down the last survivors of this magnificent species.

Almost EXTINCT

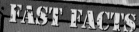

Nigel and Saba find South America's plains eerily empty of the large animals that were there when Nigel visited previously. No terror birds. No Toxodon. A drastic climate change has caused their populations to thin out to extinction. Because of the lack of prey, the remaining saber-toothed cats have been forced to spread out over large territories. To cover enough ground to find specimens for the park, Nigel and Saba decide to split up and head out on foot.

Before long, Saba gets a whiff of her first clue to finding the cats—scat! She sees evidence that a saber-toothed cat has been scraping the ground in an attempt to cover up its excrement. Nigel joins Saba as she discovers a dead cub that was about two months old. The poor thing is only skin and bones. Sadly, it died of starvation because its mother couldn't provide it enough milk. Nigel and Saba know that where there is a cub, a mother must be close by.

Saber-Toothed Cats
ON THE BRINK

As Nigel and Saba return to camp for the night, they set up a camera with a motion sensor to see if they can catch on screen a saber-toothed cat prowling around at night. While Saba sets off the next morning in search of the mother of the dead cub, Nigel checks the camera. It has been toppled by a male saber-toothed cat! Nigel follows its fresh tracks to higher ground. In the meantime, Saba has tracked the angry mother. As Saba and the saber-toothed cat face off, Saba carefully backs away.

Nigel joins Saba, and they watch the female saber-toothed cat hunt a deer. This isn't the type of prey these cats previously hunted, but they have no choice now that all the big animals are gone. The female saber-toothed cat charges the deer, but the deer easily outruns her. Saber-toothed cats were built to sprint, not run long distances. It's becoming clear to Nigel why these magnificent creatures became extinct.

Nigel and Saba follow the exhausted female back to her den. They find her picking up another cub, who does not look healthy. The mother nurses it, but it doesn't look as if the cub is getting any nourishment. How distressing!

Nigel and Saba plan to tranquilize the mother help of a dart gun, rescue the cub, and bring both to Prehistoric Park. But there's an unexpected cha plans. The feisty male who toppled the camera sh on the scene.

Nigel and Saba know that the male might try the cub, and the mother is in no position to defer Now they plan to tranquilize the male first. In ord do so, they need to get much, much closer. That' prospect! As the male saber-toothed cat comes them, Saba shoots it with the tranquilizer gun, b will take 10 minutes or so for this large cat to b sedated. In the meantime, the large, angry mal them through the jeep's windshield. Nigel and away, but it's a close call!

Once they have the subdued male loaded i truck, Nigel and Saba return for the mother a But they find that they are too late. The cub is tranquilize the mother and take her back, alor male, to Prehistoric Park. Hopefully, the pair to have their own cubs there.

Meanwhile...
BACK AT THE PARK

Look out! There's a titanosaur breakout! These restless megacreatures are able to break out of any pen Bob puts them in. No fence will hold hungry titanosaurs in search of their next meal. Bob worries that they might head out of the park gate, and he's constantly trying to head them off.

Terence and Matilda, the juvenile T. rex, still aren't getting along. The dividing wall between their pens keeps Terence safe from his larger sister, who is prone to taking her temper tantrums out on him.

During the next few weeks, Suzanne the vet spends most of her time nursing the scrawny saber-toothed cats back to health. She's optimistic that they will recover and be able to have cubs of their own.

Besides heading titanosaurs away from the park's entrance, Bob is also playing mommy to two baby Ornithomimus. They follow him everywhere! Because he was the first thing they saw when they hatched, they imprinted on him.

The next time Nigel will use the time portal, it will be to travel to a time farther back than he ever has gone before—a time when creepy crawlies ruled the world!

DID YOU KNOW?

Imprinting is common among many species of modern birds. It's a survival mechanism that ensures the chicks stay close to the first thing they see—usually their mother.

The Troodon
TAKES THE MEAT

As Nigel walks through the forest to his jeep to fetch the meat, he senses that he is being stalked. He's afraid it might be an Albertosaurus, but it turns out the stalker is something much smaller—a Troodon. A Troodon has big claws on its back legs that it uses for holding down prey while tearing off bits of meat. Soon there are several Troodon surrounding Nigel's jeep, eating the bait!

The next day, Nigel baits the wooden trap with the remaining meat. He and his crew must wait until the wind shifts, so the smell attracts the Deinosuchus in the water. The bait certainly seems to be attracting animals, but not the right ones! A Troodon shows up and takes the bait. Now there's not enough meat remaining to attract a giant croc. Nigel and his crew give up for the day and go to sleep.

Nigel is awakened the next morning by worrisome noises from the lake. An Albertosaurus has pulled down an adult Parasaurolophus, and the Deinosuchus are approaching. There will be a battle over the prey. The Albertosaurus and Deinosuchus roar at one another and play tug of war with the Parasaurolophus. Although Albertosaurus are the largest predators on land, they back down from the mighty Deinosuchus.

Out of meat, Nigel decides to use himself as bait. He splashes the water with a paddle to create vibrations. The vibrations attract a Deinosuchus, and it follows Nigel onto land and into the trap. Once trapped inside, the Deinosuchus struggles and uses its tail to knock down some of the wooden posts. Fortunately, however, reptiles tire easily. Nigel sets up the time portal, ties the rope from the trap to three of the remaining posts, and accelerates through the time portal, with the Deinosuchus in tow.

Prehistoric Park
PANDEMONIUM

Suzanne's efforts at playing cupid have paid off. There are now two saber-toothed cubs in Prehistoric Park. For some reason, though, the mother cat wasn't able to produce enough milk to feed them, so Suzanne has been playing mother as well. She's bottle-feeding the cubs. Once the cubs have been hand fed, the mother will have nothing to do with them. If they were put back in with her, they might be in danger. Suzanne has her hands full until they are weaned and begin to eat.

Martha, the mammoth, has problems of her own. The elephant matriarch has had a calf, and Martha is trying to help look after it. Becoming an "aunt" is her way of trying to gain the acceptance of the herd. However, the matriarch is being aggressive toward Martha, driving her away. Once again, Martha is by herself and lonely.

The terror birds like to take dust baths up against the fences of their pen. Doing this scrapes away enough dirt from around the fence posts that they are able to escape under the fence. They've already done it twice. Bob and his team don't have enough time to replace the fence. They are struggling with the demands of taking care of so many temperamental prehistoric animals.

The park's biggest residents, the titanosaurs, have enormous appetites. Bob has figured out that to keep them well fed, he needs to plant 2,000 trees a year!

Fortunately, Bob built the Deinosuchus pond just beyond the time portal, so Nigel doesn't have far to lure this massive creature. It's safely in its new home under the

water. As Bob drives away from the Deinosuchus pond, a creature suddenly appears from under the canopy inside the jeep. Bob screams and swerves, scaring a titanosaur. A stowaway Troodon jumps out of the jeep and takes off. Bob talks to Nigel on his walkie-talkie to alert him to the chaos that is taking place.

The panicking titanosaur is trampling the other animals' pens, and they are escaping! The terror birds are free. Bob is trying to round up the Ornithomimus and sees that Matilda the T. rex is on the loose. She's heading toward the elephants. Matilda has managed to separate the baby elephant from the herd. Martha, the mammoth, blocks Matilda's path, protecting the baby elephant.

Nigel diverts Matilda's attention, and she decides to go for the smaller but easier-to-catch meal, Nigel! As he runs past the Deinosuchus pond, the crocodile bursts out of the water to attack Matilda, slowing her down. Nigel is one step ahead and manages to climb a ladder, with Matilda snapping at his foot. He locks her in her pen.

Prehistoric Park brings in much-needed extra keepers to manage the work. The animals are soon all back in their pens. Suzanne has weaned the saber-toothed cubs. Martha is finally accepted into the elephant herd because she saved the calf's life. And Bob deals with the stowaway Troodon. The park's back under control . . . at least until Nigel's next adventure!

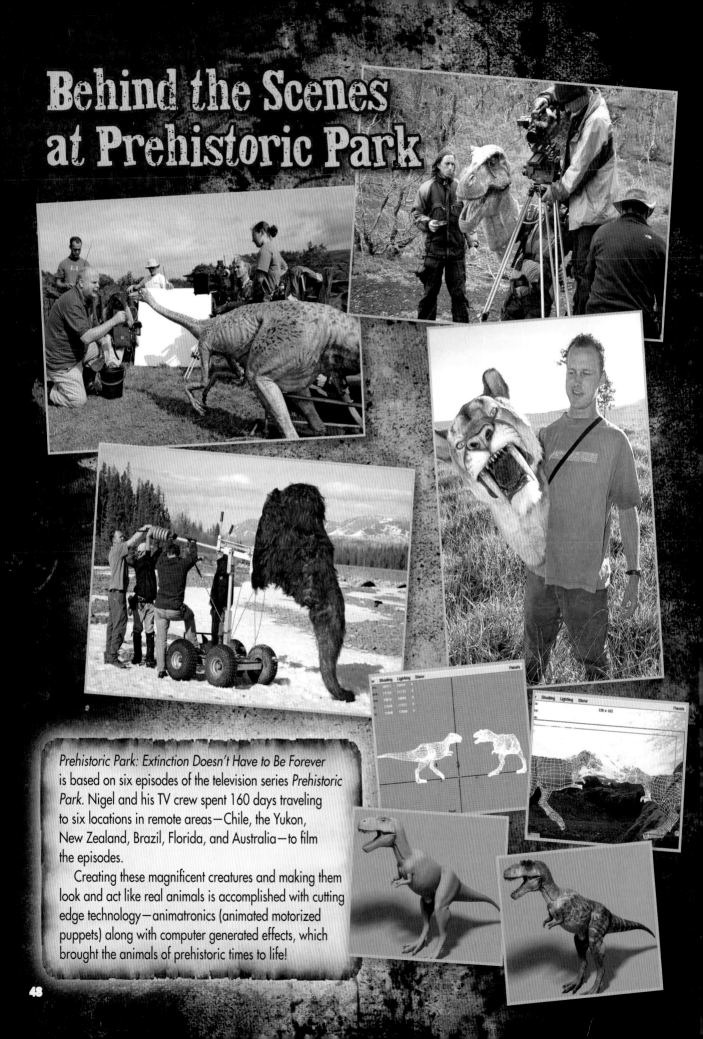

Behind the Scenes at Prehistoric Park

Prehistoric Park: Extinction Doesn't Have to Be Forever is based on six episodes of the television series *Prehistoric Park*. Nigel and his TV crew spent 160 days traveling to six locations in remote areas—Chile, the Yukon, New Zealand, Brazil, Florida, and Australia—to film the episodes.

Creating these magnificent creatures and making them look and act like real animals is accomplished with cutting edge technology—animatronics (animated motorized puppets) along with computer generated effects, which brought the animals of prehistoric times to life!